JAN 2012

P9-CBQ-152

Stark County District Library
www.StarkLibrary.org
330.452.0665

DISCARDED

PURPLE

By Patricia M. Stockland
Illustrated by Julia Woolf

Content Consultant
Susan Kesselring, MA
Literacy Educator and K-1 Teacher

magic
wagon

(COLORS)

visit us at www.abdopublishing.com

Published by Magic Wagon, a division of the ABDO Publishing Group, 8000 West 78th Street, Edina, Minnesota 55439. Copyright © 2011 by Abdo Consulting Group, Inc. International copyrights reserved in all countries. All rights reserved. No part of this book may be reproduced in any form without written permission from the publisher.

Looking Glass Library™ is a trademark and logo of Magic Wagon.

Printed in the United States of America, North Mankato, Minnesota.
092010
012011

 THIS BOOK CONTAINS AT LEAST 10% RECYCLED MATERIALS.

Text by Patricia M. Stockland
Illustrations by Julia Woolf
Edited by Nadia Higgins
Series design by Nicole Brecke
Cover and interior layout by Emily Love

Library of Congress Cataloging-in-Publication Data
Stockland, Patricia M.
  Purple / by Patricia M. Stockland ; illustrated by Julia Woolf.
    p. cm. — (Colors)
  ISBN 978-1-61641-139-8
  1. Purple—Juvenile literature. 2. Colors—Juvenile literature. I. Woolf, Julia. II. Title.
  QC495.5.S7738 2011
  535.6—dc22
                        2010013992

Our uncle puts on his chef's hat.

The hat is purple.

My brother and I put on our aprons.

The aprons are purple.

My brother gets a large pot.

The pot is purple.

7

I get the sweet grapes.

The grapes are purple.

Our uncle adds the ripe plums.

The plums are purple.

My brother and I pour in a little juice.

The juice is purple.

We tell our uncle not to add the eggplant!

The eggplant is purple.

15

16

I set fresh flowers on the table.

The flowers are purple.

Our uncle puts cake on our plates.

The plates are purple.

We taste our warm sauce.

The sauce is purple.

What Is Purple?

There are three primary colors: red, blue, and yellow. These colors combine to create other colors. Red and blue together will make purple.

Primary Colors

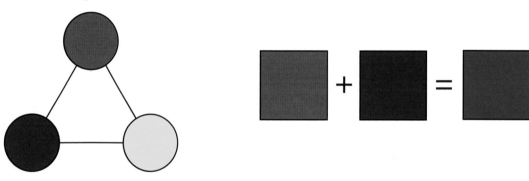

How many purple things can you find in this book?

Words to Know

apron—a covering worn to keep clothes from getting dirty.

chef—a person who is a skilled cook and manages a kitchen in a restaurant.

eggplant—a large, dark purple vegetable that is shaped like a pear.

plum—a small, round fruit with a pit in the middle.

Web Sites

To learn more about the color purple, visit ABDO Group online at **www.abdopublishing.com**. Web sites about the colors are featured on our Book Links page. These links are routinely monitored and updated to provide the most current information available.

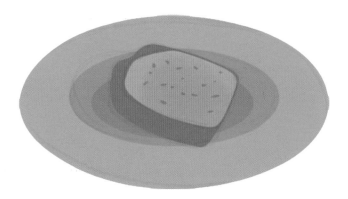